1995

Poems One Line & Longer

*Other collections of short,
short poems by William Cole*

Poems
One Line
& Longer

William Cole

Grossman Publishers
New York   1973

Contents

Introduction

There's a sentence in John Barth's *The Sot-Weed Factor* that grabbed me: "There's many a deed smells sweet at night that stinks in the heat of the sun." When I read that I said, why, it's a poem as well as a truth! I have since come across a number of one-liners that were intentionally written as complete poem; thus my title.

When I first mentioned the title to my editor, his reaction was, "That certainly covers everything, doesn't it?" And so I thought, until a few weeks later the man who runs my favorite poetry magazine, *Hearse*, sent me two issues of *Matchbook*—a magazine of one-*word* poems. These are mimeographed booklets, one poem to a page, cleverly stapled into—guess what?—matchbooks. The editor, Joyce Holland, out of Iowa City, sends copies to poets with the invitation, "Any word for us?" Somehow I can't take it seriously as poetry, although George Mattingly's contribution, "feltit," has a certain raffish charm.

To those skeptics who doubt that there can be such a thing as a one-line poem, I ask, what is a poem? Definitions abound. One old-fashioned dictionary tells me that it is "a metrical composition, esp. of elevated character." *Way* out of step. Another says "an arrangement of words . . . in a style more imaginative than ordinary speech." But of course. The quotation books have dozens of further definitions: Coleridge's "the best words in their best order," Shelley's "the record of the best and happiest moments of the best and happiest minds." You could call it beautiful shorthand; a poem is a concentrated observation; a good poem confirms your suspicions, as does a successful novel.

None of the definitions say that a poem has to be of any specified length; a poem is a statement, and what counts is how tellingly that statement is made.

Many fine poems are really only one sentence long, but are laid out longer, as D. H. Lawrence's "Tourists": "There is nothing to look at any more, / everything has been seen to death." Almost any Haiku—a form I dislike—is a broken-down sentence: "The ginko tree petal / rode on the pond surface / like a flower boat," or some such rot.

I first realized that there could be such a thing as a one-line poem when I came across five in Yvor Winters' *Collected Poems*. Then, more recently, I discovered a little book, *But Is It Poetry? An Anthology of One Line Poems*, edited by Duane Ackerson. Good stuff, and I've looted from it.

Straw for the Fire, a posthumous selection from the notebooks of Theodore Roethke, is full of one-line poems. They weren't *intended* as one-line poems, but were written down as phrases and sentences for possible later use or development. I think the ones I've used in this book stand up as entities—as poems.

But enough about one-line poems; they're only part of this collection, whose theme is really "shorter than sonnets"—poems up to and including thirteen lines. There are all manner of poems here, including a number of true-blue epigrams (definition: "a short poem ending in a witty turn of thought"). The poems are in strict form, loose form, and no form; they're vulgar, funny, outrageous, delicate, sad—all things poems should be. But, as is well known, brevity is the soul of it. My hope is that they'll get a reaction: a laugh, a sigh, a scream, a snort—something. To quote from Roethke's notebooks: "On small poems: a thing may be small but it need not be a cameo; it may be a cinder in the shoe or in the mind's eye or a pain in the neck."

William Cole

1

"Love made these poems"

Love's own form
                is sufficient unto
itself: never ask how or why:
purpose puffs a grape, in its purple hue,
packs apples; winged maples fly;
horses dogs deer run wordlessly
perfectly; the hand in love
moves through its own country:
love has no use for less than love:
love made these poems. I don't know why.

R. G. VLIET

A Word to Husbands

To keep your marriage brimming,
With love in the loving cup,
Whenever you're wrong, admit it;
Whenever you're right, shut up.

OGDEN NASH

My Dad and Mam They Did Agree

Fifty years and three
Together in love lived we;
Angry both at once none ever did us see.
This was the fashion
God taught us, and not fear:—
When one was in a passion
The other could forbear.

ANONYMOUS

The Couple Upstairs

Shoes instead of slippers down the stairs,
She ran out with her clothes

And the front door banged and I saw her
Walking crookedly, like naked, to a car.

She was not always with him up there,
And yet they seemed inviolate, like us,
Our loves in sympathy. Her going

Thrills and frightens us. We come awake
And talk excitedly about ourselves, like guests.

HUGO WILLIAMS

One Year Later

For weeks, of course, the phone still rang for you;
Letters arrived with your name and my address;
Your weight stayed long in the chairs, and even now
Something of you in the mirror changes my face.

ERIC TORGERSON

False Luve, And Hae Ye Played Me This?

False luve, and hae ye played me this,
    In the simmer, mid the flowers?
I sall repay ye back agen,
    In the winter mid the showers.

But again, dear luve, and again, dear luve,
    Will ye not turn again?
As ye look to ither women,
    Sall I to ither men.

OLD SCOTTISH SONG

From the Notebooks

Another woman: a change of tears.

THEODORE ROETHKE

How totally unpredictable we are to one another
How if all is fair in love and war
I want to begin immediately.

ROBERT SWARD

Escapist's Song

The first woman I loved, he said—
Her skin was satin and gold.
The next woman I loved, he said—
Her skin was satin and gold.
The third woman I loved, he said—
Was made in a different mold.
She was deeper than me, and said so;
She was stronger than me, and said so;
She was wiser than me, and proved it;
I shivered, and grew cold.
The fourth woman I loved, he said—
Her skin was satin and gold.

THEODORE SPENCER

Who Would Have Thought That Face of Thine

Who would have thought that face of thine
    Had been so full of doubleness.
Or else within those crystal eyne
    Had rest so much unstableness?
Thy face so fair, thy look so strange,
Who would have thought so full of change?

THOMAS HOWELL

Past Time

I believe we came together
Out of ignorance not love,
Both being shy and hunted in the city.
In the hot summer, touching each other,
Amazed at how love could come
Like a waterfall, with frightening force
And bruising sleep. Waking at noon,
Touching each other for direction,
Out of ignorance not love.

HARVEY SHAPIRO

Song

I lately vow'd, but 'twas in haste,
    That I no more would court
The Joys which seem when they are past
    As dull as they are short.

I oft to hate my Mistress swear,
    But soon my weakness find;
I make my oaths, when she's severe,
    And break 'em when she's kind.

JOHN OLDMIXON

To a Lost Sweetheart

When Whistler's Mother's picture frame
　　　Split, that sad morn, in two,
Your tense words scorched me like a flame—
　　　You shrieked, *"Ah, glue! Get glue!"*

O glue! O God! there was not glue
　　　Enough in all the feet
Of all the kine the wide world through
　　　To hold you to me, Sweet!

DON MARQUIS

Do You Love Me?

Love? I'd rather be condemned to Grand Opera,
Crammed in those little seats, that muck in my ears.
I'm too sensitive for love. The act of love
Repeats itself, repeats itself. And you?
Without my glasses are much like the last.
This bed scrambling of limbs is commonplace
As plates of breakfast eggs. Our flesh is comic.
Such odd handles, pouches, spouts, and pipes
That twitch, swell, or spurt. Like dish washing,
Done, then time to start again.
Dignity?
Animals have it over man.

ROBERT WATSON

Love Me and Never Leave Me

Love me and never leave me,
Love, nor ever deceive me,
And I shall always bless you
If I may undress you:
　　　Which I heard a lover say
　　　To his sweetheart where they lay.

He, though he did undress her,
Did not always bless her;
She, though she would not leave him,
Often did deceive him;
　　　Yet they loved, and when they died
　　　They were buried side by side.

RONALD MCCUAIG

Slave Marriage Ceremony Supplement

Dark an' stormy may come de wedder;
I jines dis he-male an' dis she-male togedder.
Let none, but Him dat makes de thunder,
Put dis he-male an' dis she-male asunder.
I darefore 'nounce you bofe de same.
Be good, go 'long, an' keep up yo' name.
De broomstick's jumped, de worl's not wide.
She's now yo' own. Salute yo' bride!

BLACK FOLK RHYME

I am yours & you are mine so
just as soon as we stop fainting over our good fortune
we will cover each other with little attentions

MICHAEL SILVERTON

When You're Away

When you're away, I'm restless, lonely,
Wretched, bored, dejected; only
Here's the rub, my darling dear,
I feel the same when you are near.

SAMUEL HOFFENSTEIN

You Say You Love Me

You say you love me, nay, can swear it too;
But stay, sir, 'twill not do.
I know you keep your oaths
Just as you wear your clothes,
While new and fresh in fashion;
But once grown old,
You lay them by,
Forgot like words you speak in passion.
I'll not believe you, I.

ROBERT HEATH

10

When We First Met

When we first met we did not guess
That Love would prove so hard a master;
Of more than common friendliness
When first we met we did not guess.
Who could foretell this sore distress
This irretrievable disaster
When first we met?—We did not guess
That Love would prove so hard a master.

ROBERT BRIDGES

Song

False though she be to me and Love,
    I'll ne'er pursue Revenge;
For still the Charmer I approve,
    Tho' I deplore her Change.

In Hours of Bliss we oft have met,
    They could not always last;
And though the present I regret,
    I'm grateful for the past.

WILLIAM CONGREVE

Pining for Love

How long shall I pine for love?
　　　How long shall I sue in vain?
How long like the turtle dove,
　　　Shall I heartily thus complain?
Shall the sails of my heart stand still?
　　　Shall the grists of my hope be unground?
Oh fie, oh fie, oh fie,
　　　Let the mill, let the mill go round.

FRANCIS BEAUMONT

Query

How
Then,
Distinguish
(Since they look
　　　　　The same)
The flush
Of pleasure
From
The Blush
Of shame?

MILDRED WESTON

2

"I think I could turn and live with animals"

Animals

I think I could turn and live with animals, they are so placid
                     and self-contained;
I stand and look at them long and long.
They do not sweat and whine about their condition;
They do not lie awake in the dark and weep for their sins;
They do not make me sick discussing their duty to God;
No one is dissatisfied—no one is demented with the mania of
                     owning things;
No one kneels to another, nor to his kind that lived thousands
                     of years ago;
No one is respectable or industrious over the whole earth.

WALT WHITMAN

Cat at the Cream

Jean, Jean, Jean,
The cat's at the cream,
Suppin wi her forefeet,
And glowrin wi her een!

SCOTTISH FOLK RHYME

15

Song

Where I walk out
to meet you on the
cloth of burning
fields

the goldfinches
leap up about my
feet like angry
dandelions

quiver like a
heartbeat in the
air and are
no more

YVOR WINTERS

The Dalliance of the Eagles

Skirting the river road, (my forenoon walk, my rest)
Skyward in air a sudden muffled sound, the dalliance of the
        eagles,
The rushing amorous contact high in space together,
The clinching interlocking claws, a living, fierce, gyrating
        wheel,
Four beating wings, two beaks, a swirling mass tight grappling,
In tumbling turning clustering loops, straight downward falling,
Till o'er the river poised, the twain yet one, a moment's lull,
A motionless still balance in the air, then parting, talons loosing,
Upward again on slow-firm pinions slanting, their separate
        diverse flight,
She hers, he his, pursuing.

WALT WHITMAN

Late at Night

Falling separate into the dark
the hailstone yelps of geese pattered
through our roof; startled we listened.

Those V's of direction swept by unseen
so orderly that we paused. But then
faltering back through their circle they came.

Were they lost up there in the night?
They always knew the way, we thought.
You looked at me across the room: —

We live in a terrible season.

WILLIAM STAFFORD

welcome

this is how to come in
not like Hamlet, hangdog
but an ENTRANCE
looking the hens over
strut
crow
make some light in the leaves

cock of the morning
to you friends
cock o' the morning

HARVEY FEINBERG

For a Little Girl Mourning Her Favorite Cat

Bathsheba! to whom none ever said scat—
No worthier cat
Ever sat on a mat,
Or caught a rat.
Requiescat!

JOHN GREENLEAF WHITTIER

Crows

I love crows.
If I met one human size
I'd invite him into my living room
and offer him the softest chair.
Then we'd crack a fifth of Old Human
and talk late into the night.
The room would be filled
with the shine and rustle of his feathers
and the wit of his sharp eye.

WILLIAM WITHERUP

The Experiment with a Rat

Every time I nudge that spring

                    a bell rings

and a man walks out of a cage
assiduous and sharp like one of us
and brings me cheese.

              How did he fall
                into my power?

CARL RAKOSI

Poem to a Mule, Dead Twenty Years

Traded by my father in a drunken rage
you died later in the yard of the processing plant.
I thought of you in the guts of hounds
circling the sedge, threading the trees at night
you, sly nibbler,
driving the fury along their veins.

No statues are raised to mules
(not even animal crackers),
but I would have it known
how once we commanded dead fields
and they answered, gold or green.

GUY OWEN

Whale Song

The pitch was lowered, slowed, decoded.

THE WORLD IS WIDE, were the words we heard,
MY SHE-LEVIATHAN BEAUTIFUL . . .
PLEASE . . . LITTLE FISH THAT WALK . . .

PLEASE . . .

FRANCIS MAGUIRE

Hens

Beside the horse troughs, General Grant
swaggered and foraged in the dry manure,
that winter we had twenty-seven hens
graced with white feathers and the names of heroes.

Cock of the walk, he took the choicest fodder,
and he was totem, stud and constable
until his comb and spurs were frozen, bled,
and then the hens—quite calmly—pecked him dead.

ALDEN NOWLAN

History Lesson for My Son

This is the way it was at Uncle Rob's
when I was young: toads. Toads under the porch
came hopping out when somebody told a joke
and everybody laughed so hard the glider
banged the house. Out came those toads hop hop
across the moonlight on the flagstones hop
into the long dark clean wet quiet grass
around my feet, my bare feet, where they lay.

TED KOOSER

The Palomino Stallion

Though the barn is so warm
that the oats in his manger,
the straw in his bed
seem to give off smoke—

though the wind is so cold,
the snow in the pasture
so deep he'd fall down
and freeze in an hour—

the eleven-month-old
palomino stallion
has gone almost crazy
fighting and pleading
to be let out.

ALDEN NOWLAN

The Dodo

The dodo was (perverse distinction)
Immortalized by his extinction.

EDWARD LUCIE-SMITH

21

Sudden Assertion

I watched the house, and barked agreeably, and
                        wagged my tail, and ran to pick up sticks
you threw with such a gesture!
You liked me when I grinned my wide approval,
although there was a red light in my eye
that made you wonder . . . and I slavered so!
Anyway, now you know,
you and the tender lambies,
now you know!

KENNETH LESLIE

Horses

And some are sulky, while some will plunge.
(So ho! Steady! Stand still, you!)
Some you must gentle, and some you must lunge.
(There! There! Who wants to kill you?)
Some—there are losses in every trade—
Will break their hearts ere bitted and made,
Will fight like fiends as the rope cuts hard,
And die dumb-mad in the breaking-yard.

RUDYARD KIPLING

22

Landscape, Deer Season

Snorting his pleasure in the dying sun,
The buck surveys his commodious estate,
Not sighting the red nostrils of the gun
Until too late.

He is alone. His body holds stock-still,
Then like a monument it falls to earth;
While the blood-red target-sun, over our hill,
Topples to death.

BARBARA HOWES

Confrontation

The mantis with translucent grin
climbs up the wrack of his six awkward limbs.

So on my palm he settles,
vein to colder vein,
stares from a steep face, bony as a stallion's
at my enormous focus:

the simple and the chambered eye.

JOHN HART

By Night

After midnight I heard a scream.
I was awake. It was no dream.
But whether it was bird of prey
Or prey of bird I could not say.
I never heard that sound by day.

ROBERT FRANCIS

On a Cock at Rochester

Thou cursed Cock, with thy perpetual Noise,
May'st thou be Capon made, and lose thy Voice,
Or on a Dunghill may'st thou spend thy Blood,
And Vermin prey upon thy craven Brood;
May Rivals tread thy Hens before thy Face,
Then with redoubled Courage give thee chase;

May'st thou be punish'd for St. *Peter's* Crime,
And on *Shrove-tuesday*, perish in thy Prime;
May thy bruis'd Carcass be some Beggar's Feast,
Thou first and worst Disturber of Man's Rest.

SIR CHARLES SEDLEY

Hope

At the foot of the stairs
my black dog sits;
in his body,
out of his wits.

On the other side
of the shut front door
there's a female dog
he's nervous for.

She's the whole size
of his mind—immense.
Hope ruling him
past sense.

WILLIAM DICKEY

The Mule

get up under a mule
sometime and look   you

may have heard wrong:
the equipment's all there

dormant   dreaming
of some great mythical

union between species
like Leda & her Swan

or the God-Bull & Europa:
the mule is an aristocrat, one

of the last Classical allusions
in this illiterate world

COLEMAN BARKS

Atossa

Cruel, but composed and bland,
    Dumb, inscrutable and grand,
So Tiberius might have sat
    Had Tiberius been a cat.

MATTHEW ARNOLD

x54, 637

The Giant Tortoise

The giant tortoise had a look
Two centuries back, at Captain Cook;

And now he has a look at you—
But is there any change of view?

For both, to him, are creatures which
Suffer from a consuming itch

For change and motion. Now, you are here;
Yet in a wink you disappear.

Such flickering things can scarcely be
A ripple in his reverie.

EDWARD LUCIE-SMITH

3

"In poetry everything is permitted"

Young Poets

Write as you will
In whatever style you like
Too much blood has run under the bridge
To go on believing
That only one road is right.

In poetry everything is permitted.

With only this condition, of course,
You have to improve the blank page.

NICANOR PARRA

Translated from the Spanish by Miller Williams

The Poet

From witty men and mad
All poetry conception had.

No sires but these will poetry admit:
Madness or wit.

This definition poetry doth fit:
It is witty madness, or mad wit.

Only these two poetic heat admits:
A witty man, or one that's out of's wits.

THOMAS RANDOLPH

To Alfred Tennyson

I entreat you, Alfred Tennyson,
Come and share my haunch of venison.
I have too a bin of claret,
Good, but better when you share it.
Though 'tis only a small bin,
There's a stock of it within.
And as sure as I'm a rhymer
Half a butt of Rudesheimer.
Come: among the sons of men is one
Welcomer than Alfred Tennyson?

WALTER SAVAGE LANDOR

Epigram on Miltonicks
After the Manner of the Moderns

What makes You write at this odd Rate?
Why, Sirs, it is to imitate.
What makes You rant and ramble so?
Why, 'tis to do as others do.
But there's no Meaning to be seen:
Why, that's the very Thing I mean.

SAMUEL WESLEY

The Muse

The Muse came pulling off her gown
and nine feet tall she laid her down
and I by her side a popinjay
with nothing to say. Did she mean to stay?

She smelled like a flame, like starch on sweat,
like sperm; like shame; like a launderette.
No one, she said, *has loved me right.
Day and night. Day and night.*

BARRY SPACKS

W. C. W.

knew a poet
doesn't have to be on
his best behavior

all the time, has
many bad
poems, very
life-like, very

relaxed, and breaks
into song
only on occasion

as all folks do,
walking along

DAVID RAY

Paradox

There are some things which, left unsaid, are true,
but become false when spoken, though there are words
for them. I mean that poetry is man's
true job, that it creates the world, and this:
that what counts in a poem is brevity.

BENJAMIN K. BENNETT

Every critic in the town
Runs the minor poet down
Every critic—don't you know it?
Is himself a minor poet.

ROBERT F. MURRAY

Past Ruin'd Illion Helen Lives

Past ruin'd Illion Helen lives,
　　Alcestis rises from the shades;
Verse calls them forth; 'tis verse that gives
　　Immortal youth to mortal maids.

Soon shall Oblivion's deepening veil
　　Hide all the peopled hills you see,
The gay, the proud, while lovers hail
　　These many summers you and me.

WALTER SAVAGE LANDOR

A Poet's Household
Three for Ted Roethke

The stout poet tiptoes
On the lawn. Surprisingly limber
In his thick sweater
Like a middle-aged burglar.
Is the young robin injured?

She bends to feed the geese
Revealing the neck's white curve
Below her coiled hair.
Her husband seems not to watch,
But she shimmers in his poem.

A hush is on the house,
The only noise, a fern
Rustling in a vase.
On the porch, the fierce poet
Is chanting words to himself.

CAROLYN KIZER

The Traditional Grammarian As Poet

Haiku, you ku, he,
She, or it kus, we ku, you
Ku, they ku. Thang ku.

TED HIPPLE

GUILLAUME APOLLINAIRE

Translated from the French by Michael Benedikt

Discontents in Devon

More discontents I never had
  Since I was born, than here;
Where I have been, and still am sad
  In this dull Devonshire:
Yet justly too I must confess;
  I ne'er invented such
Ennobled numbers for the press
  Than where I loathed so much.

ROBERT HERRICK

Epitaph

Here lies a poet, briefly known as Hecht,
Whose verse was damned for being "too correct"
By diverse rhapsodes whose unlettered song
Was fluent and conspicuously wrong.

ANTHONY HECHT

Poetry Today

The sun is eclipsed; and one by one
The birds stop singing—
Folded their wings:

But I never heard
That the frogs stopped croaking.

JOHN HEATH-STUBBS

Seven

the basic themes of lyric poetry are seven
the first one is the pubis of a maiden
then the full moon the pubis of the sky
a small stand of trees bowed down with birds
a sunset like a picture post card
the musical instrument they call a violin
and the absolute marvel of a bunch of grapes.

NICANOR PARRA

Translated from the Spanish by Miller Williams

A Poem

a poem moves down a page

faster than a novel

RICHARD MELTZER

The Relish of the Muse

The relish of the Muse consists in rhyme:
One verse must meet another like a chime.
Our Saxon shortness hath peculiar grace
In choice of words fit for the ending-place,
Which leaves impression in the mind as well
As closing sounds of some delightful bell.

SIR JOHN BEAUMONT

To Art

I loved thee ere I loved a woman, Love.

DANTE GABRIEL ROSSETTI

I begin with words of air but delightful ones.

SAPPHO

Translation by Bill Zavatsky

Ultimate Anthology

Jacket it winsomely in primrose yellow!
Here A, B, C are drained of words they said—
Decently wild now, each a handsome fellow,
With X, and Y, and charming little Z.

MARTIN BELL

4

"I wish I knew the names of all the stars"

Stars

I wish I knew the names of all the stars.
But I know only the nearest or brightest, and the others
frighten me sometimes—

not you, old Orion, many-buckled hunter,
nor you, Sirius, cross-eyed hound,
nor you, Aldebaran, bloodshot eye of the bull;

I can pull you down
into the matchbox of my mind.

But I wish I knew
the names of the others.

I would say them aloud now as I walk
alone through the woods and down to the frozen river.

ALDEN NOWLAN

The Aspen's Song

The summer holds me here.

YVOR WINTERS

Stone and the Obliging Pond

Bull's Eye: the water cries out.

FELIX POLLAK AND DUANE ACKERSON

The Haystack

Too dense to have a door,
Window or fireplace or floor,
They saw this cottage up,
Huge bricks of grass, clover and buttercup
Carting to byre and stable,
Where cow and horse will eat wall, roof and gable.

ANDREW YOUNG

Serenade

Thou moon, like a white Christus hanging
At the sky's crossroads, I'll court thee not,
Though travellers bend up, and seek thy grace.
Let them go truckle with their gifts and singing,
I'll ask no favors of thy cocker face.

Moonlight's a viand sucked by the world's lover,
Captains and peasants, all that are young and have luck.
They take the moon. Nobody asked them to.
Let the musicians lout to thee for favors;
Personally, I have other things to do.

KENNETH SLESSOR

I dreamed I saw the crescent moon
Shining, two-horned, above my bed.
I woke, and found no light was shed,
There was no crescent moon.

I lay, and felt the darkness grow.
Moaning, I felt me numb and chilled.
I looked, and saw the room was filled
With Dawn. I watched it grow.

ANONYMOUS

From the Notebooks

Deep in their roots, all flowers keep the light.

THEODORE ROETHKE

Alpine

About mountains it is useless to argue,
You have either been up or you haven't;

The view from half-way is nobody's view.
The best flowers are mostly at the top

Under a ledge, nourished by wind.
A sense of smell is of less importance

Than a sense of balance, walking on clouds
Through holes in which you can see the earth

Like a rich man through the eye of a needle.
The mind has its own level to find.

R. S. THOMAS

The Sunflowers

"Bring me a long sharp knife for we are in danger;
I see a tall man standing in the foggy corn
And his high, shadowy companions."—"But that is no stranger,
That is your company of sunflowers; and at night they turn
Their dark heads crowned with gold to the earth and the dew
So that indeed at daybreak, shrouded and silent,
Filled with a quietness such as we never knew,
They look like invaders down from another planet.
And now at the touch of light from the sun they love"—
"Give me the knife. They move."

DOUGLAS STEWART

I Meant To Tell You

I meant to tell you about the cracked birches
bent double to the ground,
iced over as if glassed around.

I meant to tell you about the snow
crushed beneath my skis
but then my breath began to freeze.

I meant to tell you . . .

SEAN HALDANE

A Bulb

Misshapen, black, unlovely to the sight,
    O mute companion of the murky mole,
You must feel overjoyed to have a white
    Imperious, dainty lily for a soul.

RICHARD KENDALL MUNKITTRICK

My Garden
With a Stern Look at T. E. Brown

A garden is a *lovesome* thing? What rot!
Weed plot,
Scum pool,
Old pot,
Snail-shiny stool
In pieces; yet the fool
Contends that snails are not—
Not snails! in gardens! when the eve is cool?
Nay, but I see their trails!
'Tis very sure *my* garden's full of snails!

J. A. LINDON

Prayer for Fine Weather

Saint Joseph, Saint Peter, Saint Paul!
Encounter the rain that it stops:
Saint Patrick, whatever befall
Keep an eye on the state of the crops!

Saint Andrew, Saint John, and Saint James,
Preserve us from deluge and floods:
If the Fiend takes to watery games,
Have pity at least on the spuds.

SHANE LESLIE

Moon Rock

Nightlong you lie and mock the idle moon
Calling it lover's lantern . . .

And calm, the vessel of the night
Slides down the sky. Now men upon her mountains
Survey their dying.

II

Men walk on that shining thing!
Never.
Call your hounds up, lady.

E. LOUISE MALLY

Knife and Sap

The pruners are quick and cruel
where life throttles life,
and settle each branchy duel
with one squeeze of the knife.

But the sap fears no knife,
the sap goes quietly stealing
to the maimed and halted life
with warm tears for healing.

KENNETH LESLIE

The Invention of Astronomy

The eyelids fall, the star-charts.

WILLIAM MATTHEWS

The stars, the stars everlasting are fugitives also.

RALPH WALDO EMERSON

Rain

The gentleness of rain was in the wind.

PERCY BYSSHE SHELLEY

From the Notebooks

I would be with the wind, in the thump and slam of this
summer joy.

THEODORE ROETHKE

Marigold

This is the plaza of Paradise.
It is always noon,
and the dusty bees are dozing
like pardoned sinners.

JOHN HAINES

Beside a Fall

Beside a fall there is a round wood pipe,
Capacious in dimension as a trunk,
That carries the dashing water to a mill.
But it is sprung with leaks. The water jets
In arcs and loops at almost every point.
The old cask is more sieve than case
To the delight of children and of me
Who come to watch the bursting seams
Of rusty iron-banded rings.
We like the little accident
Of fantastic ornament. . . .

JEAN GARRIGUE

Our Vegetable Love Shall Grow

Shaking in white streetlight in
a cold night wind, two luminous blue fangs
push through the grass at the bus shelter:
an early crocus, drawing color from
some hidden underfoot bulb. And now, mindless
desperate lonely waiting in a fen wind, we
barely move in our great coats, while that
blue piece of adventuring
takes all the electric of human light into
the beauty of its present flesh.

ELAINE FEINSTEIN

Rain

Like a drummer's brush,
the rain hushes the surface of tin porches.

EMANUEL DIPASQUALE

Small Song

The reeds give
way to the

wind and give
the wind away

A. R. AMMONS

North Labrador

A land of leaning ice
Hugged by plaster-grey arches of sky,
Flings itself silently
Into eternity.

"Has no one come here to win you,
Or left you with the faintest blush
Upon your glittering breasts?
Have you no memories, O Darkly Bright?"

Cold-hushed, there is only the shifting of moments
That journey toward no Spring—
No birth, no death, no time nor sun
In answer.

HART CRANE

A Mill

Two leaps the water from its race
    Made to the brook below,
The first leap it was curving glass,
    The second bounding snow.

WILLIAM ALLINGHAM

5

"O why was I born with a different face?"

O Why Was I Born with a Different Face?

O why was I born with a different face?
Why was I not born like the rest of my race?
When I look, each one starts! when I speak, I offend;
Then I'm silent & passive & lose every Friend.
Then my verse I dishonor, My pictures despise,
My person degrade & my temper chastise;
And the pen is my terror, the pencil my shame;
All my Talents I bury, and dead is my Fame.

I am either too low or too highly priz'd;
When Elate I am Envy'd, When Meek I'm despis'd.

WILLIAM BLAKE

Nude Descending a Staircase

Toe upon toe, a snowing flesh,
A gold of lemon, root and rind,
She sifts in sunlight down the stairs
With nothing on. Nor on her mind.

We spy beneath the bannister
A constant thresh of thigh on thigh—
Her lips imprint the swinging air
That parts to let her parts go by.

One-woman waterfall, she wears
Her slow descent like a long cape
And pausing, on the final stair
Collects her motions into shape.

X. J. KENNEDY

The Poet Asleep

                              z
                      z
                          z
richardmartinlebovit

RICHARD LEBOVITZ

The Farmer

1.
As he learned the land,
the animals came easy, goats, puppy dogs,
antelope.

2.
Animals regarded him
as a misplaced person,
his shaggy hair, his blue eyes.

3.
The wife rubbed herself with bear grease & waited.

TERRY STOKES

Hypnopompic Poem

Somehow
I cannot think of god
as the upper case.

That is a convention
I cannot attend.

WILLIAM COLE

Three Parts from
Song for Seven Parts of the Body

3.
I have a life of my own
he says. He is transformed
without benefit of bone.
I will burrow, he says,
and enters. Afterward
he goes slack as a slug.
He remembers little.
The prince is again a frog.

5.
They have eyes that see not.
They straddle the valley of wishes.
Their hills make their own rules.
Among them are bobbers
melons, fishes
doorknobs, spools.
At times they whisper, touch me.

7.
These nubbins
these hangers-on
hear naught.
Wise men
tug at them in thought.
Lovers
may nibble each other's.
Maidens
gypsies and peasants
make holes in theirs
to hang presents.

MAXINE KUMIN

The Toad-Eater

What of earls with whom you have supped,
    And of dukes that you dined with yestreen?
Lord! a louse, sir, is still but a louse,
    Though it crawl on the curls of a queen.

ROBERT BURNS

In Detroit

In Detroit, I walk out Woodward Avenue
In search of pawn shops.

I long for the easy availability
Of second-hand musical instruments.

I am drunk on the thought
Of possessing someone's discarded oboe.

Already I hear my incredible solos
Drifting up and down Woodward Avenue.

R. R. CUSCADEN

MANICdepressant

SOMETIMES I'M HAPPY;
    sometimes i'm sad;
SoMeTiMeS i'M HsAaPdPY.

KIM DAMMERS

The man that hails you Tom or Jack,
And proves by thumps upon your back
How he esteems your merit,
Is such a friend, that one had need
Be very much his friend indeed
To pardon or to bear it.

WILLIAM COWPER

The Carpenter

I am the man who
made the bed that
I must lie in;
a curious carpenter.

MICHAEL PERKINS

On Hurricane Jackson

Now his nose's bridge is broken, one eye
will not focus and the other is a stray;
trainers whisper in his mouth while one ear
listens to itself, clenched like a fist;
generally shadowboxing in a smoky room,
his mind hides like the aching boys
who lost a contest in the Panhellenic games
and had to take the back roads home,
but someone else, his perfect youth,
laureled in newsprint and dollar bills,
triumphs forever on the great white way
to the statistical Sparta of the champs.

ALAN DUGAN

The Egotist

Himself is all he'll talk about to you,
A subject that, for him, has never cloyed,
Thus furnishing an unimpeded view
Into a vast, reverberating void.

H. A. C. EVANS

Crooked Carol

Mary had a baby:
good news!
Red as a ruby,
but no layette, no shoes.

Who's to be godfather?
Joseph, maybe,
Solemn, he nods
his step-paternity

over the rude crib.
How refuse?
Mary had a baby:
Sing Whose, Whose!

NORMA FARBER

58

Barbarians

They do not come with furred caps,
Smelling of maresmilk, scimitared,
Dour, as tellable as kites.

They live quietly next door,
Speak almost the same language,
Wear almost the same clothes.

Inside the walls. But
Do not think they lack
Precisely the same intentions.

JOHN FOWLES

"Stereo"

I can clear a beach or swimming pool without
         touching water.
I can make a lunch counter become deserted
         in less than a hour.
I can make property value drop by being seen
         in a realtor's tower.
I ALONE can make the word of God have little
         or no meaning to many
         in Sunday morning's prayer hour.
I have Power,
BLACK POWER.

DON L. LEE

The Dinner

I invited Mozart to dinner
on condition he didn't
embarrass me.
In the middle of the meal
he began weeping uncontrollably.
"You silly fuck," I screamed,
"what are you doing
in this century
if you can't take it?"

GREGORY ORR

The Travelers

Approve the traveler who never went;
Slippers and timetables supply his want.

Admire the traveler who went, and stayed,
Renewing life in some rare latitude.

Honor the traveler who went, and died,
Raised above gain or failure by the deed.

But the returning traveler with a store
Of memoirs and an ancient-mariner stare

Shall be discredited from bar to bar
And in the end account himself a bore.

JAMES REEVES

Traveling North

Gradually growing fur,
you leave your canvas shoes,
sun lotion, in the gray lockers
of Canadian bus stations.

You are at the North Pole,
magnetic. Do something,
every compass is looking at you.

JOHN WOODS

Winter

(With little money in a great city)

There's snow in every street
Where I go up and down,
And there's no woman, man, or dog
That knows me in the town.

I know each shop, and all
These Jews, and Russian Poles,
For I go walking night and noon
To spare my sack of coal.

JOHN MILLINGTON SYNGE

The Talker

One person present steps on his pedal of speech
and, like some faulty drinking fountain, it spurts
all over the room in facts and puns and jokes,
on books, on people, on politics, on sports,

on everything. Two or three others, gathered
to chat, must bear his unending monologue
between their impatient heads like a giant buzz
of a giant fly, or magnanimous bullfrog

croaking for all the frogs in the world. Amid
the screech of traffic or in a hubbub crowd
he climbs the decibels toward some glorious view.
I think he only loves himself out loud.

MONA VAN DUYN

To the Heart

I saw
a specialist   a cook
place his hand in the mouth
slide it down
through the sheep's throat
touch the beating heart
close his fist on it
and tear it out with
one jerk

yes sir
that was

a specialist

TADEUSZ ROZEWICZ
Translated from the Polish by Victor Contoski

Responses

leaving the bird house
central park zoo
a small boy asks me
mister
did you kill
all the birds?
i offer him a plastic
crackerjack prize
i ask do you know
what that is?
yes he says
what is it?

ROBERT HERSHON

Eastward to Eden

My brother came home from a Princeton club
And made my mother serve the butter
(That used to be served in a big warm glob)
Cut square and thin in a bowl of ice water.

EDGAR BOGARDUS

The Liftman

He lives unsociable, aloof,
Between the Basement and the Roof,
Conveying female bourgeoisie
To Sportswear, Hats, or Lingerie.
Devoid of hope, all passion spent,
He travels, glum, pauciloquent,
Without a smile, without a frown,
Just up and down and up and down.

H. A. C. EVANS

6

"Everyone tries to get as much sex as he can"

Nine O'Clock Thoughts on the 73 Bus

Client meeting at twelve, that lot of layabouts
Will have to be spoken up for, must tell Ann
To get a new ivy for the office, louts
I saw trying to touch her up, lovely bum
Though. Everyone tries to get as much sex as he can,
The copywriter is flushed by the client's sun.

PETER PORTER

A Bon Mot
On a lady's wedding being on the 21st of December

Returned from the opera, as lately I sat,
Indifferently chatting of this and of that,
My Chloe I asked how it entered her head
To fix on St. Thomas, of all days to wed.
To which she replied, with reason the strongest,
"Tho' shortest the day is—the night, sir, is longest."

ANONYMOUS

Cavalier Lyric

I sometimes sleep with other girls
in boudoir or cheap joint,
with energy and tenderness
trying not to disappoint.
So do not think of helpful whores
as aberrational blots;
I could not love you half so well
without my practice shots.

JAMES SIMMONS

Riddle

Stiff standing on the bed,
First it's white, and then it's red.
There's not a lady in the land
That would not take it in her hand.*

OLD ENGLISH RIDDLE

*A carrot, of course [ed.]

Casanova

(buried somewhere in the cemetery at Dux in Bohemia)

No one could find his grave for relic-plunder,
      But legend said it would have paid to search
The one whose cross *would* get entangled under
      The skirts of young girls on their way to church.

RICHARD USBORNE

For Delphine

Something disturbs your big pale limbs among
White crumpled sheets, like a wave an arm
is flung
And falls; thighs, redistributed, subside
Like lifeless waves on sand, moved by a tide.
But here is something the loveliest views lack,
A pair of eyes open and stare back.

JAMES SIMMONS

The dainty young heiress of Lincoln's Inn Fields,
    Brisk, beautiful, wealthy and witty,
To the power of love so unwillingly yields,
    That 'tis feared she'll unpeople the city.
The sparks and the beaus all languish and die;
    Yet, after the conquest of many,
One little good marksman, that aims with one eye,
    May wound her heart deeper than any.

        CHARLES SACKVILLE, EARL OF DORSET

Seventh Georgic

Big black Angus bull
tries to mount one of two cows
with him in the back
of a red truck
shaking its way down the country road
to the stockyards or the slaughterhouse?
he doesn't know but keeps on
slipping on the shit on the floor
banging up against the slats
trying to make it in such crowded space
like all God's good animals
any time   any place.

        GEORGE ECONOMOU

Out of You

coming out of you
I feel like Democracy in America
slowly slipping away

RODNEY PHILLIPS

from *Themes for Country-Western Singers*

That 'lil girl that Daddy loved
has growed her a set of jugs that're droppin'
tha jaws of all the truckers
down at the EAT. She's waitin' tables
and passin' out them checks that read:
Hurry, and come right back again.

TED KOOSER

The Girl with 18 Nightgowns

and each one to the advantage of her breasts
which were present in softness
and under softness
were present
like miniature rabbits in the Andes
that only come out at night.

GREGORY ORR

At Last

At last I bless the hours
I bent to bible classes,
when I compare my bursting love
to springs responding to
the cunning rod of Moses.

ROSEMARIE NEWCOMBE

The Return

It was justice to see her nude haunches
Backing toward me again after the years,
Familiar as water after long thirst.
Now like a stream she is, and I can lie beside
Running my hand over the waters, or sleep;
But the water is colder, the gullies darker,
The rapids that threw me down have shallowed;
I can walk across.

STANLEY MOSS

The Summing Up

I understand the ties that are between us
too well to talk about the heart—that pump!
It lies between the brain-box and the penis,
and when those masters stir that slave will jump.

JAMES SIMMONS

Agatha

So she took up a number twelve crewel needle
and sewed up her box. (You could say
she had her snatch pursed.) In any case
she should have let it go at that.
Instead, she threaded out
the rest of her remaining days
needling into other lives
and wheedling out the whys and ways
of other husbands, lovers, wives.

NADINE MAJOR

Reply

Too elementary.
Sing me more than making
it between stark sheets.
That's just a punctuation
mark; I'm scratching
for the whole paragraph.

VICTORIA MCCABE

Poem

Get your tongue
out
of my mouth;
I'm kissing you
goodbye.

TED KOOSER

Behind That Wall My Roommate Fucks His Girl

I could have said makes love
but only I do that, others fuck or screw
I scowl in my corner and turn the hi fi off
to hear them better: oh tasting love
through the ears is such a painful thing:

my parts are numb as my ears stand up
attentive as trees: they are in that room
forever, bouncing gut to gut, flesh slapping
on the squeaky bed. And in my mind all the beds
I ever squeaked in, all the rooms I'd wished
I'd been in, float like pure heaven, serene
and easy, quiet in the night, disturbing no one.

GEOF HEWITT

O Terry

O Terry why is sex so quick
To make us well and make us sick.
Had we kept free of naked deeds
And I not shown my naked needs
We'd be this moment friends and pals
Instead of angry animals.

RUTH HERSCHBERGER

73

To Dianeme

Show me thy feet: show me thy legs, thy thighs,
Show me those fleshy principalities;
Show me that hill where smiling love doth sit,
Having a living fountain under it;
Show me thy waist, then let me therewithal,
By the assention of thy lawn, see all.

ROBERT HERRICK

The Rapist

I am the man crouched behind a bush
sitting at his desk.
I will never be caught. All my victims
have a way of disappearing.
No matter what sex you are,
you will be next.
You would sit next to me
at a concert performed in the woods.
If I looked at you in the subway
you would not shift your eyes.
No one ever runs. I am small, deceptive
like this poem
that is already inside you.

STEPHEN DUNN

Takes All Kinds

I figure her
for some kind
of ear freak:
every time I
tried to ease it
in her mouth
she'd turn her head
to the side.

R. P. DICKEY

The Carnation
Ode to impotence

Hail to thee
Impotence
At last women surround me
Like milk pails around a fly

At last I touch
As gently as they dreamed
I would touch them in a dream

PAUL HANNIGAN

Modern Love

She has a husband, he a wife.
What a way to spend a life!
So whenever they are free
They synchronize adultery,
And neither one would dare to stop
Without a simultaneous plop.

J. V. CUNNINGHAM

Diner

The baked potato's
hot slit's
a forward nookie:
I put butter in:
it flelts and mows:
I stick my fork in:
the white meat quivers some:
I soak my tongue in there,
eat the
quarterpound reality.

A. R. AMMONS

76

Kate Being Pleased

Kate being pleas'd, wisht that her pleasure could
    Indure as long as a buffe jerkin would.
Content thee Kate, although thy pleasure wasteth
Thy pleasures place like a buffe jerkin lasteth.
    For no buffe jerkin hath bin oftner worne
    Nor hath more scrapings, or more dressings borne.

SIR JOHN DAVIES

Human Relations

My mind is so evil and unjust
I smile in deprecation when I am flattered
But inside the palace of my smile
Is the groveling worm that eats its own tail
And concealed under the threshold of my lips
Is the trustless word that will wrong you if it can.
Come nearer to me therefore, my friend,
And be impressed by the truth of my explanation.
No less, lady, take my chaste hand
While the other imaginatively rifles your drawers.

C. H. SISSON

the adorable paratroopess alights on my throbbing spindle
all things come to him who waits

MICHAEL SILVERTON

Progress

Man is mind
cried old Descartes
and Wordsworth answered
Man is heart.

Down a new road
at last we come;
our cry: *Libido
ergo sum.*

PETER MEINKE

78

7

"With a light 'Pooh-pooh'"

Just Dropped In

Secretary of State John Foster Dulles conferred today with Burmese Premier U Nu. He said later he had come here neither to woo neutral Burma nor to be wooed. . . . His reception was studiously polite.—The New York Times.

He did not come to woo U Nu,
And there wasn't much of a state to-do,
And they sat around and talked, those two,
And there isn't a doubt that they mentioned Chou.

When reporters asked "'A political coup?"
He waved them aside with a light "Pooh-pooh."
But he didn't just come to admire the view,
Which he certainly knew *you* knew, U Nu.

WILLIAM COLE

Being Adult

A smaller role for peanut butter

BILL ZAVATSKY

Ingestion

Standing on my head makes swallowing this hot dog hard.

BARRY MCDONALD

HANDSAWWWWWWWWWWWWWWWW

RICHARD LEBOVITZ

81

One-Line Poems from a New Statesman Competition

Linger longer, Olga, prolong your vulgar conga.

MOLLY FITTON

Mine eyes have seen the guru live, by cunning, like a lord.

WASHINGTON POST

The dog howled and howled and listened and howled and howled and howled.

ALISON PRINCE

Pale faced, tight laced, ice chaste and undisgraced.

MARGARET SOUTHGATE

Human Needs
Some food, some sun, some work, some fun, some-one.

Anno Domini
An empty lap, an hour to tea, a knit, a nod, a nap, ennui.

E. M. WALKER

Dandelions
Such brazen slatterns; but later, white-haired, genteel.

GERDA MAYER

Such Is Holland!

O, land of mud and mist, where man is wet and shivers
    Soaked with humidity, with damp and chilly dew,
    O, land of unplumbed bogs, of roads resembling rivers,
Land of umbrellas, gout, colds, agues, toothache, flu,

O, spongy porridge-swamp, O homeland of galoshes,
    Of cobblers, toads, and frogs, peat diggers, mildew, mould,
Of ducks and every bird that slobbers, splutters, splashes,
    Hear the autumnal plaint of a poet with a cold.

Thanks to your clammy clime my arteries are clotted
    With blood turned mud. No song, no joy, no peace for me.
    You're fit for clogs alone, O land our forebears plotted
And, not at my request, extorted from the sea.

PETRUS AUGUSTUS DE GENESTET
Translated from the Dutch by Adriaan Barnouw

On Paunch, A Parasite

Paunch talks against good liquor to excess,
And then about his raving Patroness;
And then he talks about himself. And then
We turn the conversation on to men.

HILAIRE BELLOC

Gladstone Gave His Name to the Gladstone Bag

gladstone gave his name to the gladstone bag
and wellington is immortalised by his boot
but who remembers obadiah pinstripe
(the inventor of the pinstripe suit)?

CHRISTOPHER REID

Observation

Men *en masse*
Look a mess,
Women together
Little Better.

RICHARD WEBER

When Charlie Bowdre married Manuela, we carried them
on our shoulders, us on horses. Took them to the Shea
Hotel, 8 rooms. Jack Shea at the desk said
Charlie—everythings on the house, we'll give you the Bridal.
No no, says Charlie, don't bother, I'll hang onto her ears
until I get used to it.
HAWHAWHAW

MICHAEL ONDAATJE

University Curriculum

In this factory, here the axe-grinders
are whetted by degrees,
there are courses in log-rolling
and a shortage of trees.

WILLIAM PRICE TURNER

On Vital Statistics

"*Ill* fares the land to hastening *ills* a prey*
Where wealth accumulates and men decay."
But how much more unfortunate are those
Where wealth declines and population grows!

HILAIRE BELLOC

*This line is execrable; and I note it.
I quote it as the faulty poet wrote it. [H. B.]

English Counties

Cheshire for men,
    Berkshire for hogs,
Bedfordshire for naked flesh,
    Lincolnshire for bogs,
Derbyshire for lead,
    Devonshire for tin,
Wiltshire for hunting plains,
    And Middlesex for sin.

ENGLISH FOLK RHYME

My Aunt

I take my Aunt out in her pram
I am her grown-up Nephew "Sam"!
My Grandma's sister married late
And by a stroke of Life's strange fate
Her children all arrived when we
Were roundabout aged Twenty-three.
It is most pleasing for a chap
To bounce his Aunt upon his lap!

PEGGY WOOD

Power to the People

Why are the stamps adorned with kings
    and presidents?
That we may lick their hinder parts and
    thump their heads.

HOWARD NEMEROV

Wynken De Worde

Wynken de Worde, fyndyng thynges in a messe,
Started to prynt wyth a second-hande
Presse: "Presse
Onward and upward," he tolde hymselfe, thynkyn'
'Tis tyme that the worlde heard the worde about Wynken.

FREDERICK VON ENDE

Birds in their little nests agree
With Chinamen but not with me.

HILAIRE BELLOC

Bernard

When the completely charming
lady chairman at the meeting
introduced me as Bernard

I hardly smiled
nor was I too surprised,

having noticed while shaving
just the day before
my face in the mirror,

face of quiet resignation
of relaxed desperation

not un-saintlike.

RAYMOND SOUSTER

Glory

In the museum of antiquities
I ran my hands over
The breasts and thighs
Of the young Aphrodite
And heard her say, kiss my ass.

HARVEY SHAPIRO

A Dialogue

Pope—Since my old friend is grown so great
      As to be Minister of State,
      I'm told, but 'tis not true, I hope,
      That Craggs will be ashamed of Pope.

Craggs—Alas! if I am such a creature
      To grow the worse for growing greater;
      Why, faith, in spite of all my brags,
      'Tis Pope must be ashamed of Craggs.

ALEXANDER POPE

Positive, a Coxcomb

*("Positive is the perfection of coxcomb, he is then come
to his full growth."*

—George Savile, Marquis of Halifax, 1633–1695)

His self-conceit's so swollen by inflation
You'd make the biggest fortune ever known
If you could buy him at your valuation
    And sell him at his own.

WILLIAM PLOMER

the food drops off a fork
down a pipe
out a sphinctre
shit. Iris
enters from the garden
"1000 pardons, Rolf,
I thought you was alone."

MICHAEL SILVERTON

Postscript to Die Schöne Müllerin

The freshet springs from woodland cleft,
    Its waters crystal clear and cool;
The lovesick youth, of sense bereft,
    Leaps madly in the swirling pool.

Quelled are his turbulence and woe
    Who loved the miller's lovely daughter;
And in the village far below
    They take to filtering the water.

R. P. LISTER

Mutual Problem

Said Jerome K. Jerome to Ford Madox Ford,
"There's something, old boy, that I've always abhorred:
When people address me and call me 'Jerome,'
Are they being too formal, or too much at home?"

Said Ford, "I agree;
It's the same thing with me."

WILLIAM COLE

Epigram on the Unknown Inventor of Scissors

This Man contrived (but yet no glory won)
A Tool so singular that it had none.

L. E. JONES

I'd rather listen to a flute
In Gotham, than a band in Butte.

SAMUEL HOFFENSTEIN

And Then What?

> "I think I'll hitchhike around the country for awhile. Try to
> find myself." (overheard)

I finally ran into me one night
in a pizza joint in Albuquerque.

I was drinking Coors and
eating the red peppers. "Well kid,

here we finally are eh?
Hey Nellie, give the kid here

a drink. What'll ya have kid?"
he said.

"Coors," I said, that being
what I seemed to be

drinking.

DAVE KELLY

As in Their Time

(1)

They were so mean they could not between them
Leave one tip behind them; the others
Tipped so wildly it made no sense,
When the cold computer gathered the leavings
It broke about even, made no sense.

(III)

She believed in love, but was it
Her self or her role believed?
And was it believed and not
Professed or envied? Lastly,
Was it love she believed in?

(XI)

She was a bundle of statistics, her skin
Creamy with skinfood, *and* she knew the lingo,
So that when she entered the bush she was entirely
Camera-conscious. For all that the cannibals
Ate her one day they had nothing else to do.

LOUIS MAC NEICE

On Lady Poltagrue, A Public Peril

The Devil, having nothing else to do,
Went off to tempt My Lady Poltagrue.
My Lady, tempted by a private whim,
To his extreme annoyance, tempted him.

HILAIRE BELLOC

Lost Contact

O the vexation
of dropping
a contact lens!

The contact lens
that would help you find
the contact lens
you are looking for
is
the contact lens
you are looking for!

WILLIAM COLE

The Best Line Yet

In Stamford, at the edge of town, a giant statue stands:
An iron eagle sternly clasps the crag with crooked hands.
His pedestal is twenty feet, full thirty feet is he.
His head alone weighs many times as much as you or me.
All day, all night he keeps his watch and never stirs a feather.
His frowning brow glares straight ahead into the foulest weather.
They say this noble bird will spread his iron wings and fly
The day a virgin graduates from Stamford Senior High.
O, evil day when he shall rise above the peaceful town,
Endanger airplanes, frighten children, drop foul tonnage down!
So let not this accipiter desert his silent vigil,
But yield to me my darling, Stamford's finest, Susan Kitchell.

EDWARD ALLEN

On a Sundial

Save on the rare occasion when the Sun
Is shining, I am only here for fun.

On the Same

I am a sundial, turned the wrong way round.
I cost my foolish mistress fifty pound.

HILAIRE BELLOC

8

"Memory pressed between two pages"

Crossing

At five precisely in the afternoon
The dining car cook on the Boston and Albany
Through train to somewhere leaned and waved
At the little girl on the crossing at Ghent, New York—
The one with the doll carriage.
                              Who understood it best?
She, going home to her supper, telling her Pa?
The Negro cook, shutting the vestibule window,
Thinking: She waved right back she did? Or I,
Writing it down and wondering as I write it
Why a forgotten touch of human grace
Is more alive forgotten than its memory
Pressed between two pages in this place?

                                        ARCHIBALD MACLEISH

What It Means, Living in the City

1.
On the street-corner
across from Macy's
identical platinum blondes
twin midgets.

2.
In the parking lot at Akron
three gay boys
all deaf-mutes
camping with quick hands.

                                   WILLIAM DICKEY

The Dance

In Breughel's great picture, The Kermess,
the dancers go round, they go round and
around, the squeal and the blare and the
tweedle of bagpipes, a bugle and fiddles
tipping their bellies (round as the thick-
sided glasses whose wash they impound)
their hips and their bellies off balance
to turn them. Kicking and rolling about
the Fair Grounds, swinging their butts, those
shanks must be sound to bear up under such
rollicking measures, prance as they dance
in Breughel's great picture, The Kermess.

WILLIAM CARLOS WILLIAMS

The Night Was Smooth

Sure the night was smooth
as milkweed silk
against the fingers,
& the wet rags just washed
were warm;
even the doctor's rough farm hands
had knowing, were good.
There was a confidence.

But the baby wasn't right.

JAMES BERTOLINO

Sale

Went into a shoestore to buy a pair of shoes,
There was a shoe salesman humming the blues,
Under his breath; over his breath
Floated a peppermint lifesaver, a little wreath.

I said please I need a triple-A,
And without stopping humming or swallowing his lifesaver away
He gave one glance from toe to toe
And plucked from the mezzanine the very shoe.

Skill of the blessed, that at their command
Blue and breathless comes to hand
To send, from whatever preoccupation, feet
Implacably shod into the perfect street.

JOSEPHINE MILES

Vacation

One scene as I bow to pour her coffee: —

> Three Indians in the scouring drouth
> huddle at a grave scooped in the gravel
> lean to the wind as our train goes by.
> Someone is gone.
> There is dust on everything in Nevada.

I pour the cream.

WILLIAM STAFFORD

The Fountains

Suddenly all the fountains in the park
Opened smoothly their umbrellas of water,
Yet there was none but me to miss or mark
Their peacock show, and so I moved away
Uneasily, like one who at a play
Finds himself all alone, and will not stay.

W. R. RODGERS

The Macy's Poem

On the southwest up-escalator at the back of my mind as the
                salesbell tinkles its raindrop of cold cash,
                between floors a woman in green glances
                across at the down-escalator.
Deep in her eyes I see pinpoints of light, like raindrops rippling
                the pools of her irises, farther back than
                the eye of her brain
Till the green dress peels back revealing her skeleton, from
                egg-head to pigeon-toes, with a skeleton-grin
                but with obviously false teeth
And marks like terrible footprints on the skull from something
                like a car crash or syphilis, either of which
                might have accounted for the false teeth,
As she moves, decapitated by the fourth floor
To buy new shoes, Vaseline, a prosthetic device. . . .

But suddenly I am so tired of writing this that I, too, must get
                off the escalator, find the Beautyrest section,
                and lie down, asleep before my head hits
                the pillow.

JAMES REISS

Baptism

In summer-colored dresses, six young girls
are walking in the river; they look back,
frightened and proud; a choir and a cloud
of starlings sing; in rubber boots and black
frock-coat the preacher bends them separately
under; since the up-rushing stream expands
their skirts as they go down he closes them
each time with gently disapproving hands.

ALDEN NOWLAN

Our lives are Swiss, —
    So still, so cool,
  Till, some odd afternoon,
The Alps neglect their curtains,
  And we look farther on.

Italy stands the other side,
  While, like a guard between,
The solemn Alps,
The siren Alps,
  Forever intervene!

EMILY DICKINSON

Edwardian Hat

Standing with raised arms before
the dark face of her mirror,
hat brim a rose-pink halo
about piled hair,
she levelled the steel pin
like a rapier, then
thrust and thrust it through.

Twice the pink straw
cried out. I shuddered when
the bright point reappeared,
expecting blood.

A lifetime after she had gone
I stood at the street window,
the long pain in my head.

BETTY PARVIN

Moving

When we spurt off
in the invalid Volvo
flying its pennant of blue fumes,
the neighbors group and watch.
We twist away like a released balloon.

WILLIAM MATTHEWS

Serengeti Sunset

Miles and miles of giraffes galloping
through slow motion above the pickled bones
of Zinjanthropus, foot after foot of lions'
claws culling savannah, and lolliping,
lolliping, steps the ostrich without stooping
and leopard spots dance on the heat's muscles rippling.

Wrapped in blowsy capes the register of dung,
with tourists peeping at their genitals,
the Masai post like high cranes by their cattle.
They do not change; the sky never changes, hung
as it is with that splendid medallion,
except at sunset when it mingles milk with blood and urine.

ANDREW OERKE

New Year's Water

Here we bring new water from the well so clear,
For to worship God with, this happy New Year.
Sing levy dew, sing levy dew, the water and the wine,
With seven bright gold wires, and bugles that do shine.
Sing reign of fair maid, with gold upon her toe,
Open you the west door, and turn the Old Year go.
Sing reign of fair maid, with gold upon her chin,
Open you the east door, and let the New Year in.

WELSH FOLK RHYME

In South Wales, on New Year's morning, children go from
house to house with evergreen branches and water drawn from
a well, and sprinkle householders, singing this song. *Levy dew:*
elevation of the host. [Ed.]

How I Escaped from the Labyrinth

It was easy.
I kept losing my way.

PHILIP DACEY

The Garden Hose

In the gray evening
I see a long green serpent
With its tail in the dahlias.

It lies in loops across the grass
And drinks softly at the faucet.

I can hear it swallow.

BEATRICE JANOSCO

Old Photographs

The women are dark and seem
very beautiful; the men
look nervous, overdressed. It's always
summer where they stand,
arms linked, facing the sun,
their blurred smiles meant for no one.

DAVID HARSENT

Morning

Hollow-feeling, empty of sleep and as yet unbreakfasted,
From an already forgotten stranger's bed
I stumble out into an unfamiliar part of the town.

So dazzlingly greeted! The sunlight's sudden recognition breaking
Across a row of houses I have never seen;
These shoppers remote as if some distant generation.

Let me ask of you nothing.
All now seems possible. O let me nothing ask.

HARRY FAINLIGHT

Small Town: The Friendly

I walk Main Street, a pelican,
my jaw full of hellos.
Hello lady I don't know!
Hello everyone! I have learned
to beat them to it.
That there are things sleeping
in the most inviting doorways
no longer matters. Hello green grocer!
Hello street! Hello cold morning!
I've always wanted to do this,
and they think I'm normal.

STEPHEN DUNN

A Removal from Terry Street

On a squeaking cart, they push the usual stuff,
A mattress, bed ends, cups, carpets, chairs,
Four paperback westerns. Two whistling youths
In surplus U. S. Army battle-jackets
Remove their sister's goods. Her husband
Follows, carrying on his shoulders the son
Whose mischief we are glad to see removed,
And pushing, of all things, a lawnmower.
There is no grass in Terry Street. The worms
Come up cracks in concrete yards in moonlight.
That man, I wish him well. I wish him grass.

DOUGLAS DUNN

Cranes

Across a sky suddenly mid-February blue,
Over scaffolding that sketches where buildings are coming up,
Clearly red cranes hand out portions of concrete,
Steel girders, rubble, clumsily like cold fingers
Getting used to themselves having been numb too long.

J. R. S. DAVIES

In a Train

There has been a light snow.
Dark car tracks move in out of the darkness.
I stare at the train window marked with soft dust.
I have awakened at Missoula, Montana, utterly happy.

ROBERT BLY

Question

Where are the people
Who left their shoes
In the dusty boxes
With yellowed tags
On the bottom shelf
In the shoe shop?

NORMA CRAIG

The Past comes back in the mouth with blood.

RALPH HODGSON

The Shadow's Song

I am beside you, now.

YVOR WINTERS

9

"But O that I were young again"

Politics

"In our time the destiny of man presents its meaning in political terms."—Thomas Mann

How can I, that girl standing there,
My attention fix
On Roman or on Russian
Or on Spanish politics?
Yet here's a travelled man that knows
What he talks about,
And there's a politician
That has read and thought,
And maybe what they say is true
Of war and war's alarms,
But O that I were young again
And held her in my arms!

WILLIAM BUTLER YEATS

Heavy, Heavy—What Hangs Over?

At eighty
reading lines
he wrote at twenty

The storm now past

A gust in the big tree
splatters raindrops
on the roof

KENNETH BURKE

Age?

It can't happen to me.
We lose the image of youth
Painfully,
As if tearing the bandage
From an incurable wound.

H. R. HAYS

When First My Way to Fair I Took

When first my way to fair I took
    Few pence in purse had I,
And long I used to stand and look
    At things I could not buy.

Now times are altered: if I care
    To buy a thing, I can;
The pence are here and here's the fair,
    But where's the lost young man?

—To think that two and two are four
    And neither five nor three
The heart of man has long been sore
    And long 'tis like to be.

A. E. HOUSMAN

Turn the Key Deftly

We turn out the light to undress by,
can no longer bear the witness
of bodies that have shivered through
too many winters. We are more coy now
than ten or fifteen years ago, do not show
ourselves proudly. Sometimes when you catch my eye
I do a comedian shuffle, acknowledging the joke
about my loud paunch, the profile of my buttocks.

Side by side under kind covers we try
to push the heavy years away, resurrecting
for a moment an afternoon beside a pond.
Yet, sophisticated, prefer to joke,
allowing sleep to do our dreaming for us.

EDWIN BROCK

Tara Is Grass

The world hath conquered, the wind hath scattered like dust
Alexander, Caesar, and all that shared their sway:
Tara is grass, and behold how Troy lieth low—
And even the English, perchance their hour will come!

Translated from the Irish by Padraic Pearse

The Coming of Wisdom with Time

Though leaves are many, the root is one;
Through all the lying days of my youth
I swayed my leaves and flowers in the sun;
Now I may wither into the truth.

WILLIAM BUTLER YEATS

Gently, Years, gently!

RALPH HODGSON

Out of the Past

Where now the high-rise-village highways
sprawl, there was in other days
a picnic, woods, daisies, creek
you—someone?—waded, holding up a skirt.

ROBERT WALLACE

Behold the child, by Nature's kindly law,
Pleas'd with a rattle, tickled with a straw:
Some livelier play-thing gives his youth delight,
A little louder, but as empty quite:
Scarfs, garters, gold, amuse his riper stage,
And beads and pray'r-books are the toys of age:
Pleas'd with this bauble still, as that before;
'Till tir'd he sleeps, and Life's poor play is o'er.

ALEXANDER POPE

Invasion on the Farm

I am Prytherch. Forgive me. I don't know
What you are talking about; your thoughts flow
Too swiftly for me; I cannot dawdle
Along their banks and fish in their quick stream
With crude fingers. I am alone, exposed
In my own fields with no place to run
From your sharp eyes. I, who a moment back
Paddled in the bright grass, the old farm
Warm as a sack about me, feel the cold
Winds of the world blowing. The patched gate
You left open will never be shut again.

R. S. THOMAS

The Invisible Man

The girl who felt my stare and raised her eyes
Saw I was only an old man, and looked away,
As people do when they see something not quite nice
Or a row of houses so dreary they'll spoil your day.

Children don't see me at all: they look right through me
My sons reach out a filial helping hand
(To me, who am shaking now with lust and fury).
These facts I know but find it difficult to understand.

T. S. MATTHEWS

Organ Transplant

I drank,
my arteries filled with fat,
the ventricle went lax
and a clot stopped my heart.

Now I sit
in St. Petersburg sunshine.
No whisky.
Wearing a girl's heart.

My blood has adopted a child
who shuffles through my chest
carrying a doll.

J. D. REED

A Drinking Song

Wine comes in at the mouth
And love comes in at the eye;
That's all we shall know for truth
Before we grow old and die.
I lift the glass to my mouth,
I look at you, and I sigh.

WILLIAM BUTLER YEATS

The Fragment

Towards the evening of her splendid day
Those who are little children now shall say
(Finding this verse), "Who wrote it, Juliet?"
And Juliet answer gently, "I forget."

HILAIRE BELLOC

Middle-Aged Conversation

"Are you sad to think how often
        You have let all wisdom go
For a crimson mouth and rounded
        Thighs and eyes you drowned in?" "No."

"Do you find this level country,
        Where the winds more gently blow,
Better than the summit raptures
        And the deep-sea sorrows?" "No."

A. S. J. TESSIMOND

Into My Heart an Air That Kills

Into my heart an air that kills
        From yon far country blows:
What are those blue remembered hills,
        What spires, what farms are those?

That is the land of lost content,
        I see it shining plain,
The happy highways where I went
        And cannot come again.

A. E. HOUSMAN

10

"I am <u>Woman</u> as Heaven made Me"

Song

With my frailty don't upbraid Me,
I am *Woman* as Heaven made Me,
Causeless, doubting, or despairing;
Rashly trusting, idly fearing;
    If obtaining
    Still complaining;
    If consenting,
    Still repenting;
    Most complying
    When denying;
And, to be follow'd only, flying.
With my frailty don't upbraid Me,
I am *Woman* as Heaven made Me.

WILLIAM CONGREVE

Poem

I meet Mother on the street,

    She hardly recognizes me;
    I have to pull her by the sleeve of her coat.

    Then she stops, smiles and says:
    I'm so proud of you my son!

LENNART BRUCE

Rosy Apple, Lemon or Pear

Rosy apple, lemon or pear,
Bunch of roses she shall wear;
Gold and silver by her side,
I know who will be the bride.
Take her by the lily-white hand,
     Lead her to the altar;
Give her kisses,—one, two, three,—
     Mother's runaway daughter.

ENGLISH CHILDREN'S GAME RHYME

Kiss'd Yestreen

Kiss'd yestreen, and kiss'd yestreen,
Up the Gallowgate, down the Green.
I've woo'd wi' lords, and woo'd wi' lairds,
I've mool'd wi' carles and mell'd wi' cairds,
I've kiss'd wi' priests—'twas done i' the dark,
Twice in my gown and thrice in my sark.
But priest nor lord nor loon can gie
Sic kindly kisses as he gae me.

NINETEENTH-CENTURY SCOTTISH SONG

Gallowgate: Glasgow
mool'd, mell'd: made love
carles: common men
cairds: tinkers
sark: chemise

The Conscience

Deadly destructive to my man and me
Are my rare fits of sore morality.
A mad, domestic hell begins
When woman hides her virtues, and displays her sins.

ANNA WICKHAM

My cat and i

Girls are simply the prettiest things
My cat and i believe
And we're always saddened
When it's time for them to leave

We watch them titivating
(that often takes a while)
And though they keep us waiting
My cat & i just smile

We like to see them to the door
Say how sad it couldn't last
Then my cat and i go back inside
And talk about the past.

ROGER MC GOUGH

Treat the woman tenderly, tenderly.
Out of a crookéd rib God made her, slenderly, slenderly.
Straight and strong He did not make her,
Let love be kind, or else ye'll break her.

OLD RHYME

The nakedness of women is the work of God.

WILLIAM BLAKE

123

a woman came to me. a woman spoke to me in woman
O how awful it was for me (a man does not really understand
woman). I despaired
suddenly then angels came to me linked like sausage
it was terrible for me all over again

MICHAEL SILVERTON

you fit into me
like a hook into an eye

a fish hook
an open eye

MARGARET ATTWOOD

The Convent

The rooks above the convent walls
Are mating in the trees.
The nuns, within the convent gloom
Are praying on their knees.
O nuns upon your bended knees,
How can you really hope to please
The god of sky and sun and breeze,
Of mating birds, and burgeoning trees
By praying on your bended knees
Within a darkened room.

SEUMAS O'SULLIVAN

Epigram

The world is full of care, much like unto a bubble;
Women and care, and care and women, and women and care
        and trouble.

REV. NATHANIEL WARD

Rivalry

The nurse, who is neither young nor pretty,
warms the cold lotion with the friction of her palms,
massages my flesh as though coaxing a tired lover,
leans so close I can tell her belly is without fat,
      her breasts firm and, perhaps, beautiful

and smiles mysteriously across my naked body
at my wife, who holds my hand in both of hers,
her own smile becoming tighter and tighter.

ALDEN NOWLAN

O My Belly

O my belly, my belly, John Trench!
What's the matter with your belly, my wench?
Som'at in my belly goes niddity-nod,
What can it be, good God, good God.

ENGLISH FOLK RHYME

Social Studies

Woody says, "Let's *make* our soap,
It's easy.
We learned about it
In school."
He told Mother,
"All you do is
Take a barrel.
Bore holes in the sides,
And fill it with straw.
Ashes on top—"

"No," said Mother.

MARY NEVILLE

To a Lady

The enchantress Circe, with a potent wine,
Transformed her hapless lovers into swine;
But you, dear lady, it occurs to me,
Have not the slightest need of sorcery.

J. B. MORTON

Miscarriage

A stunned cabin boy
Steering your ship to the bottom,

A flayed finger
Attached almost to the palm of her hand,

A tea leaf
Washed from the rim of her cup,

Unembraceable, indisposable,
My son or my daughter.

MICHAEL LONGLEY

Volcanic Venus

What has happened in the world?
the women are like little volcanoes
all more or less in eruption.

It is very unnerving, moving in a world of smouldering volcanoes.
It is rather agitating, sleeping with a little Vesuvius.

And exhausting, penetrating the lava-crater of a tiny Ixtaccihuatl
and never knowing when you're going to provoke an earthquake.

D. H. LAWRENCE

Cloe

Cloe's the wonder of her Sex,
    'Tis well her Heart is tender;
How might such killing eyes perplex
    With Virtue to defend her?

But Nature graciously inclin'd
    With liberal Hand to please us,
Has to her boundless Beauty joined
    A boundless Bent to ease us.

GEORGE GRANVILLE, BARON LANSDOWNE

Marvelous

Ah my Jill loves her nakedness
and rock 'n' roll
like a fox loves hidden places.
And Marina's teats
are my darkest lilies
(she thinks she has a colored grandpa).
O Dorothy whom I no longer know is made long
like Palestine,
I'm a wandering Jew.
And Tania flings shoes off, fresh
as a comet in the sky.
And Tania's over forty!

ALLAN KAPLAN

128

A Bagatelle

How badly and how beautifully she speaks.
Her voice is like a Sunday evening chime.
As stupid and evocative as her face,
Moving and childish as an ancient rhyme.

JAMES REEVES

Girls' Voices

An old man alone in the dark, muttering
Over and over again of all foolish things his name.
The folly is less than it seems; old and alone,
He speaks his name remembering the times
He has heard it whispered by girls loving him
In oh, what a different darkness, what an age ago!
To name him then was to make him, for then, a god.
It is to girls' voices he listens and not his own.

BRENDAN GILL

Geisha

The boxer bitch is pregnant
puffed like an oriental wrestler!

The boys stand back,
aloof, embarrassed
or unsure of their hands.

But the girls, their cheeks aflame,
are down on shiny knees
praising all the nipples.

GARY GILDNER

A Song

My name is sweet Jenny, my age is sixteen
My father's a farmer on yonder green:
He's plenty of money to dress me in silk
But nae bonnie laddie will tak' me a walk.

I rose in the morning, I looked in the glass
I said to myself: What a handsome young lass!
My hands by my side and I gave a ha ha
But nae bonnie laddie will tak' me awa'.

SCOTTISH STREET RHYME

Cophetua

Oh! The King's gane gyte,
Puir auld man, puir auld man,
An' an ashypet lassie
Is Queen o' the lan'.

Wi' a scoogie o' silk
An' a bucket o' siller
She's showin' the haill coort
The smeddum intil her!

HUGH MACDIARMID

gyte: mad
ashypet lassie: kitchen maid
scoogie: apron
smeddum: gumption

Calculating Female

Her smiling eyes in the glass
Glimmer as she undresses
But what is so amusing
He neither cares nor guesses

As, centered on one elbow,
He stares at her glowing breast.
She calculates, she reckons
How fierce his interest.

Her luminous eyes mirror
What her shrewd thoughts assess
Before his arms encompass
The sweet comptometress.

JILL HELLYER

The Romantic

Virtuous, witty, proud and gay,
She found her easy conquests sweet—
Then flung her weapons all away
To learn the rapture of defeat.

COLIN ELLIS

Epigram on Two Ladies

Which is the best to hit your taste,
Fat pork or scrag of mutton?
The last would suit an invalid,
The first would gorge a glutton.

If fat and plenty is your aim,
Let Phillis be your treat;
If leaner viands are your choice,
You Pamela may eat.

SOPHIA BURRELL

Mothers and Daughters

The cruel girls we loved
Are over forty.
Their subtle daughters
Have stolen their beauty;

And with a blue stare
Of cool surprise,
They mock their anxious mothers
With their mothers' eyes.

DAVID CAMPBELL

Good Advice

Be plain in dress, and sober in your diet,
In short, my deary, kiss me, and be quiet.

LADY MARY WORTLEY MONTAGU

Her summary of a longer didactic poem sent her by Lord
Lyttleton, beginning with the line "The councils of a friend,
Belinda, hear . . ."

All I Ask—

All I ask of a woman is that she shall feel gently towards me
when my heart feels kindly towards her,
and there shall be the soft, soft tremor as of unheard bells
                            between us.
It is all I ask
I am so tired of violent women lashing out and insisting
on being loved, when there is no love in them.

D. H. LAWRENCE

11

"Yet this will go onward the same"

In Time of "The Breaking of Nations"

I

Only a man harrowing clods
    In a slow silent walk
With an old horse that stumbles and nods
    Half asleep as they stalk.

II

Only thin smoke without flame
    From the heaps of couch-grass;
Yet this will go onward the same
    Though Dynasties pass.

III

Yonder a maid and her wight
    Come whispering by:
War's annals will fade into night
    Ere their story die.

THOMAS HARDY

We Let It Go That He Was a Perfect Man

we let it go that he was crucified
we even say that he arose from the dead
—no sweat about that—
what I'd like to get cleared away
is what happened to the toothbrush
somehow or other we have to find it.

NICANOR PARRA
Translated from the Spanish by Miller Williams

POEM COMPOSED IN ROGUE RIVER PARK, GRANTS PASS, OREGON, AFTER WAYMAN'S CAR STOPPED DEAD ON THE OREGON COAST IN THE MIDDLE OF A HOWLING RAINSTORM AND HAD TO BE TOWED FIRST TO YACHATS, OREGON, WHERE IT COULDN'T BE FIXED AND THEN ONE HUNDRED MILES THROUGH THE MOUNTAINS TO EUGENE, WHERE AFTER IT WAS REPAIRED AND WAYMAN STARTED OUT AGAIN HIS ACCELERATOR CABLE PARTED AND HE HAD TO RUN ON THE LAST DOZEN MILES OR SO INTO GRANTS PASS AT MID-NIGHT WITH HIS THROTTLE JAMMED OPEN AND SPEND THE NIGHT WAITING FOR THE GARAGE TO OPEN WHICH IS AT THIS MOMENT WORKING ON HIS CAR, OR RATHER WAITING FOR A NEW PART TO BE SHIPPED DOWN FROM EUGENE (AND WHICH GARAGE, INCIDENTALLY, WOULD FIX THE CABLE BUT FAIL TO DISCOVER THAT ALL THAT HIGH-REV RUNNING WOULD HAVE BLOWN THE HEAD GASKET ON WAYMAN'S CAR CAUSING FRIGHTENING OVER-HEATING PROBLEMS THE NEXT DAY WHEN WAYMAN DID TRY TO BLAST ON DOWN TO SAN FRANCISCO)

Let me not go anywhere,
Let me stay in Grants Pass, Oregon, forever.

TOM WAYMAN

From the Notebooks

The grandeurs of the crazy man alone,
Himself the middle of a roaring world.

THEODORE ROETHKE

The Lift

The fact of this man having made
improper advances, while disturbing you,
has at the same time
given you a lift.

After ten years of marriage
something else needs to be supplied.

Good for morale
bad for morals:

the French probably have
an expression for it.

RAYMOND SOUSTER

The Fortunes of War

The fortunes of war, I tell you plain,
Are a wooden leg—or a golden chain.

ANONYMOUS

Diseases of the Moon

I have to stop answering yes and no
even to simple yes-or-no questions because
the way I live puts time in short supply
and I prefer to spend what little I have
pondering issues of inordinate complexity.

Two fairly typical examples of the recent
conclusions I have made are that the moon
is affected by the tides instead of the
other way around and that funerals ought
somehow to protest death rather than merely
acquiesce.

DOUG FETHERLING

Rooming House

The blind man draws his curtains for the night
and goes to bed, leaving a burning light

above the bathroom mirror. Through the wall,
he hears the deaf man walking down the hall

in his squeaky shoes to see if there's a light
under the blind man's door, and all is right.

TED KOOSER

Ovid in the Third Reich

*non peccat, quaecumque potest
    pecasse negare,
solaque famosam culpa professa
    facit.**

> (*Amores, III, xiv*)

I love my work and my children. God
Is distant, difficult. Things happen.
Too near the ancient troughs of blood
Innocence is no earthly weapon.

I have learned one thing: not to look down
So much upon the damned. They, in their sphere,
Harmonize strangely with the divine
Love. I, in mine, celebrate the love-choir.

GEOFFREY HILL

*She does not sin that can deny her sin—it is only avowed
dishonor brings the fault.

From the Notebooks

I rasp like a sick dog; I can't find my life.

THEODORE ROETHKE

Big Dream, Little Dream

The Elgonyi say, there are big dreams and little dreams.
The little dream is just personal . . .
Sitting in a plane that is flying
too close to the ground. There are wires . . .
on either side there's a wall.

The big dream feels significant.
The big dream is the kind the president has.
He wakes and tells it to the secretary,
together they tell it to the cabinet,
and before you know there is war.

LOUIS SIMPSON

Sleep

O living pine, be still!

YVOR WINTERS

From the Notebooks

I'm lost in my name.

THEODORE ROETHKE

Thumb

The odd, friendless boy raised by four aunts.

PHILIP DACEY

Starry Sky

All the convicts have their roaches lit.

CHARLES SIMIC

The Silent Slain

We too, we too, descending once again
The hills of our own land, we too have heard
Far off—Ah, que ce cor a longue haleine—
The horn of Roland in the passages of Spain,
The first, the second blast, the failing third,
And with the third turned back and climbed once more
The steep road southward, and heard faint the sound
Of swords, of horses, the disastrous war,
And crossed the dark defile at last, and found
At Roncevaux upon the darkening plain
The dead against the dead and on the silent ground
The silent slain—

ARCHIBALD MACLEISH

Ah, que ce cor a longue haleine: "Ah, what a long blast this horn has." From *La Chanson de Roland* in which this incident was originally described.

Don't Steal

Don't steal; thou'lt never thus compete
Successfully in business. Cheat.

AMBROSE BIERCE

143

Charity

For Forms of Government let fools contest;
Whate'er is best administer'd, is best:
For Modes of Faith let graceless zealots fight;
His can't be wrong whose life is in the right:
In Faith and Hope the world will disagree,
But all Mankind's concern is Charity:
All must be false that thwart this One great End;
And all of God, that bless Mankind, or mend.

ALEXANDER POPE

Simultaneously

Simultaneously, five thousand miles apart,
two telephone poles, shaking and roaring
and hissing gas, rose from their emplacements
straight up, leveled off and headed
for each other's land, alerted radar
and ground defense, passed each other
in midair, escorted by worried planes,
and plunged into each other's place,
steaming and silent and standing straight,
sprouting leaves.

DAVID IGNATOW

A brick not used in building
Can smash a window pane.
For anyone with ears to hear
Let it be said again.
A brick not used in building
Can smash a window pane.

NAOMI REPLANSKY

A Dutch Proverb

"Fire, Water, Woman, are Man's ruin!"
Says wise Professor Van der Bruin.
By flames, a house I hired was lost
Last year; and I must pay the cost.
This spring, the rains o'erflowed my ground,
And my best Flanders mare was drowned.
A slave am I to Clara's eyes;
The gipsy knows her power, and flies!
Fire, Water, Women, are my ruin;
And great thy wisdom, Van der Bruin!

MATTHEW PRIOR

Blessing Without Company

O Lawd have mussy now upon us,
An' keep 'way some our neighbors from us.
For w'en dey all comes down upon us,
Dey eats mos' all our victuals from us.

BLACK FOLK RHYME

The Art of Happiness

No Man e'er found a happy Life by Chance,
Or yawn'd it into Being, with a Wish;
Or, with the Snout of grov'ling Appetite,
E'er smelt it out, and grubb'd it from the Dirt;
An Art it is, and must be learnt; and learnt
With unremitting Effort, or be lost;
And leave us perfect Blockheads, in our Bliss:
The Clouds may drop down Titles, and Estates;
Wealth may seek Us; but Wisdom must be Sought;
Sought before All; but (how unlike All else
We seek on Earth?) 'tis never sought in vain.

EDWARD YOUNG

Autumn Begins in Martins Ferry, Ohio

In the Shreve High football stadium,
I think of Polacks nursing long beers in Tiltonsville,
And gray faces of Negroes in the blast furnace at Benwood,
And the ruptured night-watchman of Wheeling Steel,
Dreaming of heroes.

All the proud fathers are ashamed to go home.
Their women cluck like starved pullets,
Dying for love.

Therefore,
Their sons grow suicidally beautiful
At the beginning of October,
And gallop terribly against each other's bodies.

JAMES WRIGHT

The Balloon of the Mind

Hands, do what you're bid:
Bring the balloon of the mind
That bellies and drags in the wind
Into its narrow shed.

WILLIAM BUTLER YEATS

1867: Last Sounds

Three hundred from one village
left Rathlin Island in a famine. . . .

In the evening, over the waves,
howling of dogs at the empty homes. . . .

GERRY O'EGAN

Some twenty years of marital agreement
Ended without crisis in disagreement.
What was the problem? Nothing of importance,
Nothing but money, sex, and self-importance.

J. V. CUNNINGHAM

Graffiti

I drink to forget, but whenever I think
I'm happy I rejoice in drink.

ALAN BOLD

Money

I was led into captivity by the bitch business
Not in love but in what seemed a physical necessity
And now I cannot even watch the spring
The itch for subsistence having become responsibility

Money the she-devil comes to us under many veils
Tactful at first, calling herself beauty
Tear away this disguise, she proposes paternal solicitude
Assuming the dishonest face of duty.

Suddenly you are in bed with a screeching tear-sheet
This is money at last without her night-dress
Clutching you against her fallen udders and sharp bones
In an unscrupulous and deserved embrace.

C. H. SISSON

Anatomy

Certain portions of the heart
die, and are dead. They are
dead.

Cannot be exorcised or brought
to life.

Do not disturb yourself
to become whole.

They are dead, go down
in the dark and sit with them
once in a while.

GILBERT SORRENTINO

12

"I will consider the outnumbering dead"

Merlin

I will consider the outnumbering dead:
For they are the husks of what was rich seed.
Now, should they come together to be fed,
They would outstrip the locusts' covering tide.

Arthur, Elaine, Mordred: they are all gone
Among the raftered galleries of bone.
By the long barrows of Logres they are made one,
And over their city stands the pinnacled corn.

GEOFFREY HILL

Epitaph for the Tomb of Adolfo Baez Bone

They killed you and didn't tell us where they
        buried your body
but since then all our land is your tomb,
or let's say: you came back to life
                in each inch in which your body is not.

They thought they killed you with an order "fire!"
They thought they buried you
and what they did bury was a seed.

ERNESTO CARDENAL
Translated from the Spanish by Janet Brof

News

I sink my soft butt in an easy chair
and read about those killed by war,
earth-quake, disease, plane-crash, fire;
but not about my dead, or my prayed-for.

I have waited, shivering in my skin,
numb on a wooden bench from need
to hear the doctors' report on one.
One still white face brings home the news I read.

MARNIE POMEROY

Memorial Service

His aging widow dreams of youth,
his sons stand in their father's place,
his friends translate him into stone,
sisters recall his childhood face,
so quickly death confuses truth.
He lies in state, corrupt, alone.

Though hopes and fears are multiplied
boredom blunts pain and stifles doubt,
words weave a dream of light and life.
His widow rises like a bride
comes down the aisle, leads the dark rout
and greets her friends as deaths' new wife.

URSULA VAUGHAN WILLIAMS

Epitaph on Floyd

Floyd has died and few have sobb'd,
Since, had he lived, all had been robb'd;
He's paid Dame Nature's debt, 'tis said
The only one he ever paid.
Some doubt that he resign'd his breath,
But vow he's cheated even death.
If he is buried, then, ye dead, beware,
Look to your swaddlings, of your shrouds take care.
Lest Floyd should to your coffins make his way,
And steal your linen from your mould'ring clay.

ANONYMOUS

What Kind of War?

Ask what kind of war it is
where you can be pinned down
all day in a muddy rice paddy
while your buddies are being shot
and a close-supporting Phantom jet
who has been napalming the enemy
wraps itself around a tree and explodes
and you cheer inside?

LARRY ROTTMAN

On An Anniversary
After reading the dates in a book of Lyrics

With Fifteen-ninety or Sixteen-sixteen
We end Cervantes, Marot, Nashe or Green:
Then Sixteen-thirteen till two score and nine,
Is Crashaw's niche, that honey-lipped divine.
They'll say I came in Eighteen-seventy-one,
And died in Dublin . . . What year will they write
For my poor passage to the stall of night?

JOHN MILLINGTON SYNGE

Not Waving but Drowning

Nobody heard him, the dead man,
But still he lay moaning:
I was much further out than you thought
And not waving but drowning.

Poor chap, he always loved larking
And now he's dead
It must have been too cold for him his heart gave way
They said.

Oh no no no, it was too cold always
(Still the dead one lay moaning)
I was much too far out all my life
And not waving but drowning.

STEVIE SMITH

154

Prayer

Give me a death like Buddha's, let me fall
over from eating mushrooms provençal,
a peasant wine pouring down my shirt front,
my last request not a cry but a grunt;
kicking my heels to heaven, may I succumb
tumbling into a rose bush after a love
half my age. Though I'm deposed, my tomb
shall not be empty, may my belly show above
my coffin like a distant hill, my mourners come
as if to pass an hour in the country,
to see the green, that old anarchy.

STANLEY MOSS

Exit Molloy

Now at the end I smell the smells of spring
Where in a dark ditch I lie wintering—
And the little town only a mile away,
Happy and fatuous in the light of day.
A bell tolls gently. I should start to cry
But my eyes are closed and my face dry.
I am not important and I have to die.
Strictly speaking, I am already dead,
But still I can hear the birds sing on over my head.

DEREK MAHON

Beautiful Youth

The mouth of a girl who had been lying in the rushes for a
                    long time
looked so nibbled up.
When they opened the chest, the windpipe was so riddled.
Finally, in a gazebo under the diaphragm
they found a nest of young rats.
A little sister was dead.
The others had been feeding on the liver and kidneys,
drinking the cold blood and generally
having a beautiful youth.
And beautiful and quick was their death:
they were all dumped into water.
Oh, how the little muzzles squeaked.

GOTTFRIED BENN
Translated from the German by Joachim Neugroschel

Death

If death were truly conquered, there would be
Too many great-great-great-great aunts to see.

L. E. JONES

Heart Burial

They brought it along and they slipped it in,
Mr Hardy's heart in a biscuit tin,
Mrs Hardy said This grave is my bed
And my husband Tom was not well bred.

Then the heart spoke up, and mildly said
Give me to my old dog Wessex instead,
Give me to my surly dog Wessex instead.
But Wessex was busy with a fresh sheep's head,

And the rector pretended he did not hear,
The grave-digger was dry, and wanted beer,
And bumpetty bump and din din din
Earth fell on the box and the biscuit tin.

GEOFFREY GRIGSON

Orpheus in Greenwich Village

What if Orpheus,
confident in the hard-
found mastery,
should go down into Hell?
Out of the clean light down?
And then, surrounded
by the closing beasts
and readying his lyre,
should notice, suddenly,
they had no ears?

JACK GILBERT

Owls

The murderous owls off Malo bay
Can lure a sleepless watchman to the sea,
For their deep singing may be heard
Throughout a night of thunder and their red
Eyes take him dancing silently
Down to the choking sea-bed. Far away
His heavy wife sleeps like the dead
Upon the feathers of a bird.

JOHN FULLER

Epitaph

(*for 2nd Officer James Montgomerie of the* S. S. Cars-
breck, *lost at sea*)

My brother is skull and skeleton now,
Empty of mind behind the brow,
In ribs and pelvis empty space,
Bone-naked, without a face.

On a draughty beach drifting sand,
Clawed by a dry skeleton hand,
Sifts in the hourglass of his head
Time, useless to bones of the dead.

WILLIAM MONTGOMERIE

Sea Shanty

"I love the sea because it has drowned me,"
    Said the sailor with the coral nose.
"I love the sea because it has fed me,"
    Said the lobster with grasping claws.

"Liquid I lived and liquid die,"
    Said the sailor with the coral nose.
"Give us this day our daily dead,"
    Said the lobster with grasping claws.

CLIFFORD DYMENT

In the Thirtieth

In the thirtieth year of life
I took my heart to be my wife,

And as I turn in bed by night
I have my heart for my delight.

No other heart may mine estrange
For my heart changes as I change,

And it is bound, and I am free,
And with my death it dies with me.

J. V. CUNNINGHAM

After Lorca

The church is a business, and the rich
are the business men.
                    When they pull on the bells, the
poor come piling in and when a poor man dies, he has a
        wooden
cross, and they rush through the ceremony.

But when a rich man dies, they
drag out the Sacrament
and a golden cross, and go *doucement, doucement*
to the cemetery.

And the poor love it
and think its crazy.

ROBERT CREELEY

The Statue

When we are dead, some Hunting-boy will pass
And find a stone half-hidden in tall grass

And gray with age: but having seen that stone
(Which was your image), ride more slowly on.

HILAIRE BELLOC

Bereft Child's First Night

I've come to close your door, my handsome, my darling
I've come to close your door and never come again.
The shadow on the ceiling will not be mine, my darling,
So if you wake in terror cry some other name.

There's first time and last, my handsome, my treasure,
No other time, nothing between.
So whenever the hand of darkness clenches on your candle
Shut your eyes, my darling, and slip back into our dream.

FRANCES BELLERBY

After X-Ray

The bones are all there waiting their hour,
patient as hangers, pushed to the back of a closet,
on which this flesh is hung just for a while.
I feel them come to the surface slowly,
rise like their image in the developer's tank,
waiting to break through skin. And what can death
do with these bones? Planted like dry pods
in the earth they bloom later, washed clear of blood
to shine somewhere like strung beads of coral.

LINDA PASTAN

Epitaph on Any Man

I let him find, but never what he sought;
    I let him act, but never as he meant;
And, after much mislearning, he was taught,
    Tired, to be content with discontent.

A. S. J. TESSIMOND

Graffiti

The last words of Shaw: "I'm going to die."
You'd think that even a deity would wonder why.

ALAN BOLD

That Summer

That summer nothing would do
but we sink the boat
in the heart of the lake
and swim in the cool night
for the yellow fire on the beach.

Through the dark water.

We all made it but Ronald,
whom we never found,
who was never Ronald
again; each fish I catch
since, I ask, Ron, is that you?

HERBERT SCOTT

Life flows to death as rivers to the sea,
And life is fresh and death is salt to me.

J. V. CUNNINGHAM

When Daddy Died

His spirit went into the television
he'd loved so well
since the early days of the magic medium.
Sometimes, flickering through
between commercials at a station break,
we'd see a pale face, smiling,
a hand holding up a product
that hadn't been on the market for twenty years.
When we turned the knob,
the small speck sinking
into the darkness of the screen
seemed almost a personal loss.

DUANE ACKERSON

An Anarchist's Letter

Mabel—when is the bomb set to

HARALD WYNDHAM

Acknowledgements

Abelard-Schuman Limited: "Money" from *The London Zoo* by C.H. Sisson.

Cyrilly Abels: "The Invisible Man" by T.S. Matthews. Copyright © 1969 by T.S. Matthews. This poem originally appeared in *The Atlantic Monthly*.

Duane Ackerson: "When Daddy Died" by Duane Ackerson. © 1970 by Duane Ackerson.

Anansi Press, Canada: From *The Collected Works of Billy the Kid*, Michael Ondaatje © 1971; from *Power Politics*, Margaret Atwood © 1971. Reprinted by permission of House of Anansi Press.

Angus & Robertson (U.K.) Ltd.: "Mothers and Daughters" by David Campbell, "Calculating Female" by Jill Hellyer, "The Sunflowers" by Douglas Stewart, "Serenade" by Kenneth Slessor, and "Love Me and Never Leave Me" by Ronald McCuaig.

Antaeus: "Barbarians" by John Fowles. © *Antaeus,* summer 1970, New York, N.Y.

Atheneum Publishers, Inc.: "Do You Love Me?" from *Christmas in Las Vegas* by Robert Watson. Copyright © 1971 by Robert Watson. Reprinted by permission of Atheneum Publishers.

Frances Bellerby: "Bereft Child's First Night" by Frances Bellerby. Copyright © 1971 by Frances Bellerby. This poem originally appeared in *The Listener*.

171

Index of Authors and First Lines

178